In essentials unity,
in non-essentials liberty,
in all things charity.

"… without passing
judgment on disputable
matters."
Romans 14:1b

Christian Essentials

~

Book 1
God and Creation

By William C. Oakes

Published by
Eaglewing Publishing
Post Office Box 188
Warrens, Wisconsin 54666
www.eaglewingpublishing.com

Table of Contents

Note to the Class Leader

At the class leader, it is important that you lead this class and not just facilitate a discussion. Here are some suggestions on how to do that:

- Ensure that everyone has their own book to write in. Upon completion of the course, the book will make a good reference.
- Have an established class time and begin the class on time.
- Agreed to an ending time and always end on time.
- Always open and close the class with prayer.
- Allow the Holy Spirit to do His work in each person's life.
- But also be prepared by having an answer for each question.
- Study the scriptures before the class. Study cross-references to the scriptures and be especially aware of differing views and interpretations of the scriptures.
- Cover the scriptures and analysis in the book but then share what you learned in your study time.
- **Do not** require homework. The object is to fellowship together, listen to the scriptures, understand them, learn from them and each other, and record the proper response for future reference.
- How to lead each class meeting:
    - Read the scripture aloud. Start with the King James version but then read from other translations for more clarity.
    - Read aloud the commentary and briefly discuss it.
    - Read aloud each analysis question and discuss them.
    - When an answer has been agreed upon, encourage everyone to write it in their book.
- In the interests of better understanding how others in the Body of Christ interpret scripture, always have at least the following Bible translations available: King James Version, New American Standard, New International Version, and the Amplified Bible.
- Watch out for the student who likes to talk too much, or has a tendency to get off topic, or wants to debate every point.
- Encourage everyone to share their thoughts. Draw everyone into the conversation. Give the shy ones easy ways to contribute.
- Allow the Holy Spirit to dictate the pace. Don't rush but don't be boring. Keep things moving. Lead with enthusiasm! Enjoy what you are doing!

Note to the Student

As a student, it is important that you participate and not just sit and listen. The Holy Spirit will be speaking to each person in the class, including you. Therefore, it is important that each person share what they are thinking, feeling, agreeing with, and questioning.

Many times it is difficult to put your thoughts into words. There are complex issues that require us to think long and hard. Here are some suggestions for how to participate in the class:

- Rather than try to make statements, or to make a convincing argument, just ask honest questions.
- When something does not seem clear, or quite right to you, ask that the scripture be read in a different translation.
- Ask what other Christian teachers have taught about the subject?
- Ask yourself, and the class, what is the harm if we don't believe what is being taught?
- Ask someone to explain how the teaching came about in the first place. Is it a recent interpretation or has it been the same since the very beginning of the Church?
- Ask if the interpretation given is universally agreed to or is it something that only some believe? Then ask why the difference?
- Remember that the Holy Spirit wants us to use our brains, wants us to think logically, so our faith and hope are joined with our reason and intellect—not divorced from them.

This book is intended to become a part of your personal library, a reference book that you created for yourself. So make sure you write your answer to each of the analysis questions. If you miss a class, I encourage you to meet with the class leader outside of class and go over the parts you missed. The purpose of this Bible Study is to hear what the Holy Spirit would say to us from the scriptures. This works best in groups of two or more, just as Jesus Christ promised us in Matthew 18:20.

Once you have completed the Christian Essentials study series, if you have diligently applied yourself to it, you will have a well-grounded understanding of the essential Christian truths. You will be better able to accurately handle the Word of God and to share your faith with others. You will have grown past the need for spiritual milk. You will be prepared to start or expand your service in the Kingdom of God.

Christian Essentials

1. God Himself

God is One and Personal

Ephesians 1:4

Commentary: The God we worship is a thinker and a planner.

Analysis:

1. For whom, or about whom, is God's plan?

2. How long ago did God begin His plan?

3. How detailed was God's plan in the beginning?

(Read scripture in Amplified Bible and New Living Translation. Also review Thompson's Chain Reference Numerical Index #4154.)

Genesis 1:1

Commentary: God not only thinks and plans but acts upon His plans.

Analysis:

1. What does the phrase "in the beginning" mean?

2. What was going on the *day before* the beginning?

3. What existed before the beginning?

Deuteronomy 6:4

Commentary: There is only one God. Anything else is a lie.

Analysis:

1. What modern religions are mono-theistic?

2. Does God being personal mandate that He is also singular?

3. Is being 'one God' the same as being 'the only God'?

(Follow the Cross References in your Study Bibles and read the scriptures.)

God and Creation

John 3:16

Commentary: God thinks, acts, and feels—therefore God is personal.

Analysis:
1. To be personal is the opposite of what?

2. Does God have a personality? Explain.

(Compare to the deities of Buddhism, Taoism, Deism, etc.)

3. Is God a person? Explain.

4. What difference does this make, if any?

(Read in Amplified Bible. Provide dictionary definitions of 'person' and 'personality'.)

James 2:19

Commentary: The Old and New Testaments agree that there is only one God.

Analysis:

1. In context, why is there so much emphasis on this?

2. Did James believe in evil spirits / devils?

3. Are evil spirits personal too, able to think, feel, and act?

4. What does this say about spiritual beings in general?

(See Bible Topic: "One God" as in Thompson's Chain Reference #2649.)

1. God Himself

God is One in Three Persons

Genesis 1:26

Commentary: The statement "Let us make" points to more than one person in the Godhead. There is a relationship within the Godhead.

Analysis:

1. What does the term 'Godhead' signify?

2. What does 'image' (*tselem*) generally mean?

3. What does 'likeness' (*demuwth*) generally mean?

Genesis 11:7

Commentary: At the Tower of Babel is another example that the Godhead has more-than-one personality.

Analysis:

1. Does anything indicate how many personalities (persons) are present? More than one but less than ____?

2. Does one personality appear to dominate the others? At this point in God's revelation of Himself, does He differentiate?

3. In verses 6 and 8, who is the speaker?

Isaiah 6:8

Commentary: God is both "I" and "Us" but still one God.

Analysis:

1. Is this God's way of showing us He has more than one person?

2. Does the fact of God's *plurality* change anything for us? What if He were not?

3. How might a *monotheist* explain this verse?

Matthew 3:16-17

Commentary: The Trinity revealed although that word is not in the Bible.

Analysis:

1. Who are the elements of the Trinity (Tri-Unity)? In this scene, where is Jesus? The Holy Spirit? God the Father?

2. Is the "Spirit of God" a literal dove? Then why a dove?

3. Read also Matthew 28:19 and John 15:26. According to 1 Peter 1:2 what specific role does each person of the Godhead play?

Christian Essentials

1. God Himself

God the Father

Isaiah 63:16

Commentary: God has revealed Himself as our Father.

Analysis:

1. The Hebrew word for father is '*ab.*' From this we get **abba** in Romans 8:15 and other places, translated as 'Daddy'. Describe the difference between Father and Daddy.

2. Isaiah the prophet lived around 740 B.C. This was many hundreds of years after Abraham, Jacob, and Moses. Explain why the revelation of God as their Father might have been hard to accept.

3. Respond to this statement: Until the Children of Israel could accept God as a Father, they could not rightly understand the trinity.

(Don't Miss: God's revelation of Himself did not start with His being a Father and having an Only Son.)

Luke 4:3

Commentary: God has revealed Himself as a Father even to Satan.

Analysis:
1. Did Satan question whether there was such a thing as the "Son of God?"

2. If not, what was his question to Jesus?

3.Satan assumed that the Son of God would be like His Father. How is this shown in this scripture?

(Study the Jewish mind-set about the relationship between a Father and his Son.)

John 8:42-44

Commentary: God is not Father to every person on earth.

Analysis:

1. Assuming that Jesus was not playing with words, what is the clear teaching of this passage? Why is it important?

2. This scripture says that everyone has one or the other of two spiritual Fathers. Who are these two spiritual Fathers?

3. When did Satan become a Father?

4. Was it ever God's intention for angels to be fathers? Who instead was created in God's own image and likeness, and told to be fruitful and multiply (Read Genesis 1:27-28 if need be!)

1. God Himself

God the Son

Matthew 9:2-7

Commentary: Jesus Christ claims to be the same as God, to be God.

Analysis:

1. How does this scripture make the claim that Jesus Christ is God?

2. In Jesus' time and earlier, how were sins forgiven?

3. Why did the scribes get upset at Jesus? Had no man ever before said what Jesus said? If not, why not?

Matthew 18:20

Commentary: Jesus Christ claims God's omnipresence (omnipresence).

Analysis:
1. What does 'omnipresence' mean?

2. Since Jesus' body could only be in one place at a time, what was he talking about?

3. What if this were not true of Jesus? What difference might it make in a Christian's life?

John 5:22-23

Commentary: Jesus Christ claims God's right to be our judge.

Analysis:

1. Why is it significant that the scripture says that God the Father has committed all judgment to the Son?

2. Why might Jesus Christ be a "better" judge for mankind?

3. Why did God the Father make His Son our judge?

(Read this in the New Living Translation too.)

Matthew 28:20

Commentary: Jesus Christ claims to have eternal life.

Analysis:

1. Does this scripture teach that Jesus would live forever or something else?

2. This scripture not only speaks about eternal life but also omnipresence. Explain how.

3. Who does Jesus promise to be with until the end of the age?

John 8:58

Commentary: Jesus Christ claims to have been alive well before his earthly birth.

Analysis:

1. Was Jesus saying that he was alive prior to the time of Abraham, about 2,000 years earlier?

2. Or was Jesus using the great name of God "I am" to prove another point?

3. How well did Jesus know Abraham?

John 17:5, 24

Commentary: Jesus Christ claims to have been with God prior to his birth, even prior to the creation.

Analysis:

1. Was Jesus one of the "Let us make" personalities of Genesis 1:26?

2. Was Jesus also one of the "Let us go down" personalities of Genesis 11:7

John 1:1-3

Commentary: The Word was God and Jesus Christ is the Word., therefore Jesus Christ is God. Each person of the Trinity is fully God. This is a great mystery!

Analysis:

1. What was the significance of the Word during creation?

2. Compare John 1:1-3 with Genesis 1:1. Do you think John was intentionally mirroring Genesis 1?

3.Why does John use the term "Word" to describe the second person of the Trinity?

(Do a word study on the word, 'Word'.)

John 20:28

Commentary: Thomas is one of the first to see the truth that Jesus is God.

Analysis:
1. Review the history of Thomas up until his statement.

2. What did it take to convince Thomas that Jesus was God?

3. Examine the differences between the terms "Messiah," "Son of God," and "God" as they apply to Jesus Christ.

Christian Essentials

1. God Himself

God the Holy Spirit

John 15:26

Commentary: Jesus Christ describes a third person of the trinity, the Holy Spirit.

Analysis:

1. Where was the Helper at this time, and who must send Him?

2. What would the Helper do after He arrived?

3. Read John 16:7-11. How likely is it that a person can be saved without the testimony of the Helper?

(Read in the Amplified Bible too.)

God and Creation

Luke 12:10, 12

Commentary: Jesus Christ tells about the importance of the Holy Spirit.

Analysis:
1. What does it mean to blaspheme?

2. What is one of the major activities of the Holy Spirit?

3. This is called the Unpardonable Sin yet it reads that the sin "will not be forgiven." Is there any sin God can not forgive, that is impossible for Him to forgive? Perhaps Jesus did not pay the price for this sin?

(Do a word study on 'blaspheme'.)

John 16:7-14

Commentary: Jesus is going to be with God the Father but will send another person of the Godhead, a third person.

Analysis:

1. The word translated "reprove" or "convict" is *elegcho*. It also means: admonish, tell a fault, convince, rebuke. How does it differ from the word "condemn?"

2. What are the three things that the Comforter will convict the world of?

3. Who does the Comforter convict of these things? Who does he not convict?

Acts 13:2

Commentary: The Holy Spirit can also speak for himself (we use the pronoun 'he' because the Bible uses the masculine form of the pronoun).

Analysis:

1. Is the Holy Spirit merely a messenger from God? Or does he have his own thoughts, issue his own orders?

2. Read verse 4 also. The passage says they ministered to the "Lord" then the "Holy Spirit" spoke, and they were sent by the "Holy Spirit". Might this make it appear that there is more than one God to the average person?

3. Who in the Trinity is the most active person on the earth today? What are the other two doing?

4. Is it really true that we can separate them so completely?

Acts 16:6-10

Commentary: The Holy Spirit is an active participant in the lives of Christians.

Analysis:

1. Explain why it is a comfort to us that the Holy Spirit will correct us, forbid us, from going against his will?

2. How do you suppose that the Holy Spirit communicated to the apostles they were not to go into Asia or Bithynia?

3. After Paul's vision, to whom did they attribute that they were called to preach in Macedonia?

Ephesians 4:29-32

Commentary: The Holy Spirit has feelings that we can influence.

Analysis:
1. **Lupeo** is the word translated "grieve." It also means: cause to be sad, to be sorrowful, to be in heaviness, to distress. This shows that that Holy Spirit is a person and that our actions affect him. Is this true of only the Holy Spirit? What about the Father and the Son?

2. What things cause the Holy Spirit distress, sadness, and sorrow?

3. The opposite of sadness is _____. Are there things can we do that will gladden the Holy Spirit?

Christian Essentials

1. God Himself

The Trinity

2 Corinthians 1:2-3, 13:14

Commentary: The Bible clearly teaches tri-unity of the Lord God. Now that this has been revealed, to worship anything less is to worship a false god.

Analysis:
1.What clues were given to the trinity in the Old Testament? Moses wrote the book of Genesis. If he did not understand that the Godhead had more than one person, could he have written Genesis 1:26?

2. What did David believe about the Godhead according to Psalms 51:11?

3. Do you agree or disagree with the Commentary?

Romans 8:9-11

Commentary: One cannot be saved if there is no Trinity.

Analysis:

1.Some will say that these references to the "Spirit of God" are merely saying that God is a spirit, not that there is a third person. Do these verses give you that impression?

2. Christianity is all about the Holy Spirit indwelling a believer. Why is that necessary for our salvation?

3. 1 Corinthians 6:19 makes a bold statement. Where does the Holy Spirit now reside? Who placed him there?

Revelation 5:1-9

Commentary: A solitary God could not save mankind.

Analysis:
1.Why was it necessary that a "man" be found to open the book?

2. Verse 9 speaks about blood, Christ's blood. Why is blood so important to the plan of redemption?

3. Is there anyway to be saved without the blood of Jesus Christ? If one refused to believe in the trinity, is there any way left for salvation?

2. God's Creation

The Creator

Genesis 1:1

Commentary: The first attribute of God we are given is 'creator.'

Analysis:
1. What is meant by the phrase "the heavens and the earth?" How inclusive is it? Is anything not included in it?

2. "In the beginning" of what? As the start to a book, what is the topic of discussion?

3. The word translated "God" is *elohiym*. This is the plural form of the word. What does that signify?

God and Creation

Exodus 20:11

Commentary: God made all of the places and all of the inhabitants.

Analysis:

1. Much debate surrounds the meaning of "six days." Were they literally six 24 hour days? Were they six "eras" like the "acceptable year of the Lord" (Luke 4:19) was not a literal year?

2. Why do you suppose that three locations are named: heavens, earth, and sea? Or is there no obvious significance?

3. When we think about mosquitoes, poisonous insects and reptiles, and deadly animals—how can it be that God created them? And if He did not, where did they come from?

Psalm 33:6

Commentary: God created with a Word.

Analysis:

1. There are 2 ways to interpret this phrase "by the word of the Lord the heavens were made". What are they?

2. To create means to make something from nothing (read Hebrews 11:3). Why can no man ever be called the creator of anything, but only the maker of it?

3. Have you noticed that God was creator of both the material world and its inhabitants. Do you think he put as much careful attention into the one as the other? Why?

God and Creation

John 1:1-3

Commentary: And the Son of God was that Word.

Analysis:

1. John 1 reflects Genesis 1. It seems likely that the author was intentionally drawing the parallel. Why are we not surprised by this? What was the clue in Genesis 1 that prepares us for John's choice of words?

2. "He was in the beginning with God." Explain how this is possible. How the Word could have no beginning.

3. *Logos* is Greek for "Word." It means 'something said (including the thought)'. It is hard for us to think of ourselves as different from, separate from, our thoughts and spoken words. How closely connected must the Father and Son truly be?

Revelation 4:11

Commentary: God the Creator is also known as the First Cause.

Analysis:

1. This scripture tells us why God created anything. What caused Him to do it?

(See also Proverbs 16:4.)

2. Because God is our creator, He is worthy to receive what? From whom?

3. In the context of the book of the Revelation, it is important to know that God is the creator of all things and the upholder of all creation (Hebrews 1:3). What is about to happen to creation?

2. God's Creation

The Creation

Genesis 1:1-31

Commentary: God is Good and can only create Good.

Analysis:

1. In verse 4, God saw that what He had created was 'good' and all that good pertains. What are some other things that are good? Here is a start to your list: Beauty, gladness, kindness,

2. In verse 31, God saw that all of His creation <u>taken together</u> was more than good. What was it and why? Why might the whole be even better than the parts?

3. The Greek for 'very' is ***me'od***. It really means vehemently, exceedingly, especially, utterly. How do these words improve upon 'very?'

God and Creation

Genesis 3:17-18

Commentary: God is Good but also Holy.   Sin must be punished.

Analysis:
1. In God's cursing of Adam, what changed about the world around him?

2. Can we tell whether thorns and thistles had never existed before this point, or just that they were not a problem?

3. Since this is God's curse upon Adam, describe what nature might have been like before this time.

Romans 8:19-22

Commentary: God's good creation suffers.

Analysis:
1. The creation is "subject to vanity" and in "bondage to corruption." Explain what this means.

2. Who is responsible for this situation?

(See Jeremiah 12:4 too.)

3. How will it be remedied? When and by whom?

Revelation 21:1

Commentary: God's will is to restore all that was good.

Analysis:

1. The Bible speaks of the "first heaven and the first earth" as having passed away. What were these "first" places?

2. What replaces the first heaven and the first earth? When will it happen?

3. Compare with Exodus 20:11. What is missing in God's 'second' creation? Why might that be?

(Might it be because Man was created to live in heaven and on earth but not under water?)

Revelation 21:2-3

Commentary: God's will is to dwell among Mankind forever.

Analysis:

1. Where is the New Jerusalem coming down from?

2. Where is the New Jerusalem apparently going down to?

3. Therefore, where is Man destined to spend all of the rest of eternity?

4. When God created the first heaven and earth, He said it was very good. Why do you suppose so many Christians expect to spend all eternity in heaven and not on earth? Where will God be dwelling?

(Should our evangelistic message include the New Heaven and Earth in it or just about getting to heaven?)

2. God's Creation

The Purpose of Creation

Psalm 19:1-4

Commentary: Creation is a message.

Analysis:

1. The word 'firmament' means 'the visible arch of the sky.' What happens in the firmament that might show His handiwork?

2. The word for 'heavens' used here is **shamayim**. It means both the firmament and what we call space. What things are in the heavens that declare God's glory?

3. To whom is God declaring and showing Himself? Why?

(Read this scripture in the New Living Translation. What should our response to God's message be?)

God and Creation

Acts 14:15-17

Commentary: Creation is a gift.

Analysis:

1. In context, what was the point the Apostle Paul was making?

2. Today, many people try to explain the natural world in terms that ignore and deny God. How was it different in Paul's day?

3. To whom is the creation a gift? Only to Christians?

(How should we respond to God's gift?)

Romans 1:18-23

Commentary: Creation is an indictment, an accusation.

Analysis:

1. Creation is the display of God's invisible attributes. What attributes are on display?

2. What do most men do with God's revealed glory?

3. Not many people today worship carved idols of wood or stone. So does this mean that this scripture is no longer applicable? Explain.

Revelation 21:1-3

Commentary: Creation is a mystery; the chosen dwelling place of God for the everlasting future.

Analysis:

1. God is a Spirit and need no dwelling place. But is Jesus Christ a Spirit or does He have flesh and bone? (Read Luke 24:39)

2.   Compare Genesis 3:8-10 with Revelation 21:1-3. What is different?

3. Where is Mankind's (those with flesh and bone) natural dwelling place? (Read Genesis 1:31 again)

Christian Essentials

2. God's Creation

The Cursing of the Creation

Genesis 3:1-24

Commentary: All of God's promises are conditional, to be consistent with allowing Mankind a free-will. The decision to rebel against God is what caused the cursing of the creation.

Analysis:

1.   Not only was the ground suddenly going to produce troublesome thorns and thistles (weeds). Mankind was also driven from the Garden of Eden. Is it accurate to say that the Garden of Eden was cursed?

2.   Genesis 1:29-30 spells out what Mankind was originally intended to eat. What was it?

3. Did this menu change immediately after Genesis 3?

God and Creation

Genesis 9:1-4

Commentary: After the Flood, the world changed in significant ways again. The cursing seems to have progressed further.

Analysis:
1. What can we assume from this scripture with regards to Noah's dinner menu?

2. Verse 2 says that God would make animals to fear humans. Would you therefore assume that this was a new thing? Might you call this a further cursing?

3. Noah and his family were the first people authorized by God to eat meat and fish. Were there any rules on which animals could not be eaten?

4. Can we explain how there had never been a rainbow before? Or had there been?

Luke 5:4-7 and Matthew 21:18-19

Commentary: The curse seemed not to apply to Jesus.

Analysis:

1. How are we to understand these scriptures? What authority did Jesus command?

2. Are these signs of Jesus the Messiah or demonstrations of Jesus the last Adam?

3. Imagine a world where Adam's word ruled all. Why is this not so fanciful?

Revelation 21:5

Commentary: Jesus Christ, the Son of God, the Lamb of God will restore (make new) the creation.

Analysis:

1. In context with the rest of chapter 21, what is being made new? Is anything not being restored?

2. Why is it appropriate that the one who sits on the Great White Throne is the one to do this?

Accept him whose faith is weak, without passing judgment on disputable matters.

One man's faith allows him to eat everything, but another man, whose faith is weak, eats only vegetables.

The man who eats everything must not look down on him who does not, and the man who does not eat everything must not condemn the man who does, for God has accepted him.

Who are you to judge someone else's servant? To his own master he stands or falls. And he will stand, for the Lord is able to make him stand.

Romans 14:1-4 (NIV)

The Essentials Survey

Sincere Christians may disagree on certain things without harm. These are called "disputable matters" in Romans 14:1 or "non-essentials." The Apostle Paul gives clear instruction on how to deal with non-essential matters that might otherwise divide us. Is it not a command of scripture to agree on the essentials and not to argue (discuss, Yes, but not argue) about the non-essentials?

On this page, please indicate those topics you believe are beyond dispute, are absolutely essential, fundamental, mandatory to being a Christian. Compare your answers with others in the class. Be open-minded (in humility and love, demonstrating a teachable spirit) to consider another's perspective. After all, the goal is unity in the faith. Not unity at the expense of truth; but Christian unity nevertheless.

TOPIC   **ESSENTIAL**
                                                                    (Yes/No)

- The Trinity (One God in Three Persons)
- One cannot be saved without believing
- In the trinity.
- God is Father to only the Saved.
- God the Son is fully God.
- God the Holy Spirit is fully God.
- God is the Creator of all material things.
- All creation occurred in six 24-hour periods.
- The Gap Theory of creation is correct.
- Noah's ark is factual and accurate.
- Adam's sin caused all creation to be cursed as a punishment to him.
- Jesus Christ is still today fully God and fully Man (flesh and bone).
- Mankind's eternal home is with God in the New Jerusalem on the New Earth.

William C. Oakes (Bill) is Senior Pastor of Living Stones Fellowship (www.LSFW.org) and Director of "The International" (www.LSFI.org), an internet-based ministry to the Body of Christ globally.

Bill holds a BS in Liberal Arts and an MA in Christian Theology. He is also an author, columnist, teacher, and Project Management Professional.

He lives in Wisconsin with his wife and high school sweetheart, Marcie. However, they spend much of their time visiting their two grown children in Colorado.

www.ingramcontent.com/pod-product-compliance
Lightning Source LLC
Chambersburg PA
CBHW071847020426
42331CB00007B/1887